W9-AWO-832

# Dolphins/Delfines

## By Valerie J. Weber

**Reading Consultant:** Susan Nations, M.Ed.,
author/literacy coach/consultant in literacy development/

**Consultora de lectura:** Susan Nations, M.Ed.,
autora/tutora de alfabetización/consultora de desarrollo de lectoescritura

**WEEKLY READER**®
PUBLISHING

**Please visit our web site at www.garethstevens.com.**
**For a free catalog describing our list of high-quality books,**
**call 1-800-542-2595 (USA) or 1-800-387-3178 (Canada).**
**Our fax: 1-877-542-2596**

**Library of Congress Cataloging-in-Publication Data**

Weber, Valerie.
 (Dolphins. Spanish & English)
 Dolphins = Delfines / by/por Valerie J. Weber.
   p. cm. — (Animals that live in the ocean = Animales que viven en el océano)
 Includes bibliographical references and index.
 ISBN-10: 0-8368-9246-1 ISBN-13: 978-0-8368-9246-8 (lib. bdg.)
 ISBN-10: 0-8368-9345-X ISBN-13: 978-0-8368-9345-8 (softcover)
  1. Dolphins—Juvenile literature. I. Title. II. Title: Delfines.
QL737.C432W4318  2009
599.53—dc22             2008016887

This edition first published in 2009 by
**Weekly Reader® Books**
An Imprint of Gareth Stevens Publishing
1 Reader's Digest Road
Pleasantville, NY 10570-7000 USA

Copyright © 2009 by Gareth Stevens, Inc.

Senior Managing Editor: Lisa M. Herrington
Senior Editor: Barbara Bakowski
Creative Director: Lisa Donovan
Designer: Alexandria Davis
Cover Designer: Amelia Favazza, *Studio Montage*
Photo Researcher: Diane Laska-Swanke
Translation: Tatiana Acosta and Guillermo Gutiérrez

Photo Credits: Cover, pp. 1, 5, 11, 13, 15, 17, 19, 21 © SeaPics.com;
p. 7 Picture Quest; p. 9 © Jeff Rotman/naturepl.com

Printed in the United States of America

1 2 3 4 5 6 7 8 9 10 09 08

# Table of Contents

- - - - - - - - - - - -

# Contenido

**Boldface** words appear in the glossary./
Las palabras en **negrita** aparecen en el glosario.

## A Mammal, Not a Fish

Like a fish, a dolphin lives in the water.  A dolphin swims like a fish, but it is not a fish!

- - - - - - - - - - - - - -

## Un mamífero, no un pez

Un delfín vive en el agua, igual que un pez.  Pero, aunque nada como los peces, ¡un delfín no es un pez!

dolphin/
delfín

A dolphin is a **mammal**. It needs to breathe air, just as people do. A dolphin swims to the top of the water. Then the animal sucks in air through its **blowhole**.

- - - - - - - - - - - - - - -

Un delfín es un **mamífero**. Respira como las personas. Para respirar, nada hasta la superficie del agua. Allí, toma aire por medio de su **espiráculo**.

6

Like other mammals, dolphins give birth to live young. A baby dolphin is called a **calf**. A baby dolphin drinks milk from its mother's body.

- - - - - - - - - - - - - - -

Igual que otros mamíferos, los delfines paren crías vivas. Una **cría** de delfín se alimenta bebiendo leche materna.

calf/
cría

**Time for Fun**

Dolphins like to play. They race through the sea. They leap high out of the water.

- - - - - - - - - - - - - -

**Hora de divertirse**

A los delfines les encanta jugar. Echan carreras en el mar. Saltan muy alto sobre el agua.

Dolphins spin on their tails. They also flip in circles. Sometimes dolphins hit the water hard with their bellies.

- - - - - - - - - - - - - -

Los delfines giran sobre su cola. También dan volteretas. A veces, golpean el agua muy duro con la panza.

## Speedy Swimmers

Dolphins chase fish, trying to catch them. A dolphin's speed helps it catch its **prey**. Prey are animals that are hunted and eaten.

- - - - - - - - - - - - - -

## Nadadores veloces

Los delfines persiguen a los peces para atraparlos. Su velocidad permite al delfín atrapar a sus **presas**. Una presa es un animal que es devorado por otro animal.

Dolphins dig for small fish that hide under sand. A dolphin uses its strong **snout** to push at the ocean floor.

--------------

Los delfines escarban en la arena para buscar peces pequeños escondidos. Un delfín usa su fuerte **hocico** para remover el fondo marino.

snout/
hocico

Sharks often hunt for dolphins. With its sharp teeth, a shark sometimes takes a bite from a dolphin. The dolphin swims fast to escape.

-------------

A veces, los tiburones atacan a los delfines. Un tiburón puede morder a un delfín con sus afilados dientes. Para escapar, el delfín tiene que nadar muy deprisa.

shark bite/
mordedura de tiburón

19

## Making Some Noise

Dolphins often live in groups. They click and whistle to each other. Each dolphin in a group makes a different sound. It uses the same sound for its whole life.

------------------

## Un poco de ruido

Los delfines suelen vivir en grupos. Para comunicarse, emiten chasquidos y silbidos. Dentro de un grupo, cada delfín produce un sonido diferente. Hace el mismo sonido durante toda su vida.

20

# Glossary/Glosario

**blowhole:** an opening on top of a dolphin's head through which it breathes air

**calf:** a baby dolphin or other animal

**mammal:** a warm-blooded animal that has hair on its skin and that makes milk to feed its young

**prey:** animals that are eaten for food

**snout:** the front part of an animal's head, including its nose, mouth, and jaws

- - - - - - - - - - - - - - - - -

**cría:** delfín u otro animal cuando es joven

**espiráculo:** abertura en la parte superior de la cabeza de un delfín, que el animal usa para respirar

**hocico:** parte delantera de la cabeza de un animal, incluyendo la boca, la nariz y las mandíbulas

**mamífero:** animal de sangre caliente, con pelo y que produce leche para alimentar a sus crías

**presas:** animales devorados por otros animales

22

# For More Information/Más información

## Books/Libros

*Dolphins/Delfines.* Let's Read About Animals/Conozcamos a los animales (series). Kathleen Pohl (Gareth Stevens, 2007)

*What Sea Animals Eat/¿Qué comen los animales del mar?* Nature's Food Chains/Las cadenas alimentarias en la naturaleza (series). Joanne Mattern (Gareth Stevens, 2007)

## Web Sites/Páginas web

**Defenders of Wildlife/Defensores de la vida salvaje**
*www.defenders.org/wildlife_and_habitat/wildlife/dolphin.php*
Learn about different kinds of dolphins, how they grow, and what they eat./Conozcan diferentes tipos de delfines y aprendan cómo crecen y qué comen.

**Dolphins at Enchanted Learning/Delfines en Enchanted Learning**
*www.enchantedlearning.com/themes/dolphins.html*
Find quizzes, activities, and information about dolphins./ Adivinanzas, actividades e información sobre los delfines.

# Index/Índice

## About the Author

A writer and editor for 25 years, Valerie Weber especially loves working in children's publishing.  The variety of topics is endless, from weird animals to making movies.  It is her privilege to try to engage children in their world through books.

- - - - - - - - - - - - - - -

## Información sobre la autora

A Valerie Weber, que ha sido escritora y editora durante 25 años, le gusta sobre todo trabajar en libros infantiles.  La variedad de temas es inagotable: desde insólitos animales hasta cómo se hace una película.  Para ella es un privilegio tratar de interesar a los niños en el mundo por medio de sus libros.